SAFE SEX
IN A
DANGEROUS
WORLD

SAFE SEX ▬ IN A ▬ DANGEROUS WORLD

Understanding and Coping
with the Threat of AIDS

Art Ulene, M.D.

VINTAGE BOOKS
A DIVISION OF
RANDOM HOUSE
NEW YORK

Library of Congress Cataloging-in-Publication Data
Ulene, Art.
Safe sex in a dangerous world.
1. AIDS (Disease)—Popular works.
2. AIDS (Disease)—Prevention.
3. Safe sex in AIDS prevention. I. Title.
[DNLM: 1. Acquired Immunodeficiency
Syndrome—prevention & control—popular works.
2. Sex—popular works. HQ 12 U37s]
RC607.A26U44   1987   616.9′792   87-40122
ISBN 0-394-75625-8

Text design by Tasha Hall
Diagrams by Phil Scheuer

Manufactured in the United States of America
10 9 8 7 6 5 4 3 2 1

*To those who battle so bravely
against AIDS—the men, women,
and children who have the disease, and
the people who care for them.*

Michael S. Gottlieb, M.D., was the primary consultant for this book. He is credited with the first clinical description of AIDS and the first report of the new disease to the United States Centers for Disease Control in 1981. Dr. Gottlieb has been a member of the faculty of the UCLA School of Medicine since 1980. He is in the private practice of internal medicine and immunology in Santa Monica, California. He is a founder of the American Foundation for AIDS Research (AmFAR) and chairs the Scientific Policy Committee of that group.

Acknowledgments

I could not have written this book (and would not have undertaken the task) without the help of Dr. Michael Gottlieb, a dedicated scientist, a compassionate physician, and a really decent human being. On short notice, he took precious time away from his schedule (and his skiing) to grant interviews, review manuscripts, and make many helpful suggestions. I feel privileged to have worked with him.

I also want to express my appreciation to the many others who took time from busy schedules to respond to our questions and requests for information: James Allen, M.D.; Wendy Arnold; Doyne Bailey; Robert Davis; Roger Detels, M.D.; Timothy Dondero, M.D.; Jay Hartz; Martin Hirsch, M.D.; Frank Judson, M.D.; Roger Kohn; Betty McDivitt; Mead Morgan, M.D.; Dan Niebrugge; Terry P. O'Brien; Barbara Peabody; Hugh Rice; Neil Schramm, M.D.; Michael Schuster;

George Smith, M.D.; Jerry Sohli; Thomas Starcher; Paul Stolley, M.D.; Griffith Thomas, M.D., J.D.; John Ward, M.D.; Warren Winkelstein, Jr., M.D.; Gary Wood.

My thanks to Sheila Hutman, who supervised the research for the book and helped write the first draft of the manuscript. The research effort was well supported by Terry Moore and Shelley Flick, and the logistical problems were ably managed by Leslie Nadell and Pam Rabeck.

Special thanks go to Rebecca Saletan, who made the book more readable with her insightful suggestions and thoughtful editing. In spite of ridiculous deadline pressures, she worked without complaint, and I am truly grateful to her.

For all that is useful and good about this book, I must share the credit with those above. I accept complete responsibility for the rest.

Contents

SAFE SEX
IN A
DANGEROUS
WORLD

Introduction

safe ('sāf) adj 1. Not apt or able to cause or incur danger, harm, or evil; 2. Free from danger or injury; 3. Free from hazard; sure.

According to the dictionary, being safe is an "all or none" proposition—you're either safe or you're not. But that isn't the meaning most people are using when they talk about "safe sex" and AIDS.

We are told that we can have "safe sex" by using condoms, avoiding anal intercourse, giving up other forms of sexual contact that permit the exchange of body fluids, and limiting the number of our sex partners. These seem like minor inconveniences to endure for being able to continue an active sex life.

But no one talks about condom failures. And few people realize that there is a risk of infection if the one partner you limit yourself to is carrying the AIDS virus. The term "safe sex" means different things to different people, but this is a time when we cannot afford flexible definitions.

The concept of "safe sex" was initiated within the homosexual community. It was, in part, an attempt by this group to protect the health—but also the life-styles—of its members. It was also partly an attempt by bathhouse operators to protect their businesses. In retrospect, it is clear that both groups underestimated the danger of AIDS and the need for more dramatic changes in sexual behavior if the spread of this disease was to be stopped, both within the homosexual community and beyond it.

Homosexual men were not the only ones who got the "safe sex" message from posters that were put up in bathhouses. The posters were given prominent coverage by television news programs, and millions of Americans who saw them on their screens at home were left with the impression that "safe sex" was actually possible with an infected partner.

The idea of "safe sex" picked up more steam as medical journals published studies showing that AIDS-like viruses could not penetrate the walls of condoms —at least not in the laboratory. Condom manufacturers worked hard to convince the public that the laboratory results would hold for actual use by humans, although the facts suggest that condoms are—in real life—less than 100 percent effective.

It is clear that many people do not have an accurate

understanding of their risks in today's sexual world. If you are sexually active, it's critical that you do have this information as you make decisions that can affect your health—indeed, your life.

As of May 1987, almost 35,000 cases of AIDS have been reported in the United States. Already, more than 18,000 people are dead from AIDS—a disease that was virtually unknown six years ago. We are told that 291,000 people will come down with AIDS by the end of 1991, and that 180,000 people will have died of it by then. We live in a dangerous world.

AIDS is a frightening disease, but it can be avoided. The purpose of this book is to show you what you must do to avoid it. For many readers of this book, that will require absolutely no change at all in behavior. For others, it will require dramatic life-style changes and significant sacrifices.

When you finish reading this book, you will know what you must do to remain free of the AIDS virus. If you are uncertain at this time of whether you are free, I'll show you how to find out. If you are carrying the AIDS virus, I'll tell you what you can expect, and what I—as a physician—think you should do to keep others free of it.

If any of my recommendations seem extreme or unrealistic, so be it. With a disease like AIDS, the price of poor advice is so high that I cannot recommend anything less than what I believe in.

I hope this book helps you to understand AIDS better, and motivates you to protect yourself against it. I am an eternal optimist, so I believe that we will find an answer to this tragic problem in the not-too-distant future. I want you here—and healthy—when that happens.

Please don't let your education about AIDS stop with this book. Not a week passes without some change in our knowledge about this disease, so keep your eyes open for new information.

If you have personal concerns about AIDS, I urge you to discuss them with your doctor or with another qualified person whom you trust. Do not let ignorance keep you in fear. Fear will keep you in darkness, and it is darkness that can jeopardize your health and the health of those around you.

CHAPTER ONE

About AIDS

WHAT IS *AIDS*?

Acquired Immune Deficiency Syndrome (AIDS) is a viral disease that slowly destroys the body's immune system, leaving a person helpless against infections and cancers that would be turned away by the immune systems of healthy people. The virus that causes AIDS* is a fairly fragile organism. It is easily killed by heat, dilute bleach, and alcohol, and it cannot live long outside the human body without exactly the right conditions being present.

---

*By international agreement, the virus that causes AIDS has been officially named the human immunodeficiency virus (HIV). Previously, this same virus and its variants have had several names: lymphadenopathy-associated virus (LAV), human T-cell lymphotropic virus type III (HTLV-III), and AIDS-associated retrovirus (ARV). For purposes of clarity and ease of reading, I shall simply call it the AIDS virus throughout this book.

It is not easy to pass this virus from one person to another. It requires intimate, usually repeated, contacts, with exchange of infected body fluids. But once it gets inside the body, it is impossible to get rid of.

The AIDS virus is able to enter the body without causing any symptoms or warning signs. It quickly finds the way to its favored home—white blood cells known as T-helper cells. These cells play a critical role in fighting infections of all kinds. The virus inserts itself into the genetic material of these cells, duplicates itself almost endlessly through them, and thus damages the very cells that are supposed to defend against such attacks.

Like cold viruses, the AIDS virus is able to take on many slightly different shapes and forms. Unlike the cold viruses, however, it can remain silent in the body

AIDS INCIDENCE BY AGE GROUP*

Age Group	Number	(%)
Under 5	405	(1)
5–12	55	(0)
13–19	136	(0)
20–29	6,892	(21)
30–39	15,330	(47)
40–49	6,803	(21)
Over 49	3,204	(10)
	32,825	[100]

*AIDS Weekly Surveillance Report, Centers for Disease Control, March 16, 1987.

for months or years—seemingly gone or inactive—but all the while retaining its ability to infect others.

THE NATURAL COURSE OF THE DISEASE

The AIDS virus gains access to the body of one person when infected fluids like blood or semen from another person are deposited in a vulnerable or receptive area. We are still not sure how the virus actually gains access into the bloodstream. Breaks in body tissues like skin or the lining of the mouth give the virus fairly direct access to the blood. In some areas—like the anus and rectum—it is possible that the surface cells themselves can become infected, later spreading the infection to other areas through the bloodstream.

Once in the bloodstream, the virus ultimately comes in contact with the T-helper cells, where it finds a waiting home. On the surface of these cells is a receptor site that matches the unique shape of the surface of the virus. The virus attaches to this natural "landing pad" on the surface of the T-helper cell, from which it gains entry to the inside of the cell. The virus then rapidly begins to duplicate itself inside the T-helper cells.

Other T-helper cells respond by stimulating different cells of the immune system (B-cells) to make antibodies against the virus. The antibodies that are made to fight the AIDS virus are different from the antibod-

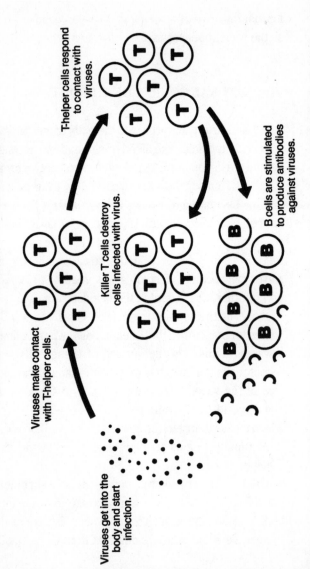

HOW YOUR BODY REACTS TO MOST VIRUSES

Viruses get into the body and start infection.

Viruses make contact with T-helper cells.

T-helper cells respond to contact with viruses.

Killer T cells destroy cells infected with virus.

B cells are stimulated to produce antibodies against viruses.

WHAT HAPPENS IN A PERSON WHO DEVELOPS AIDS

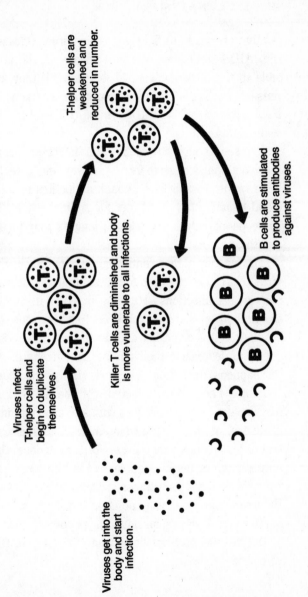

Viruses get into the body and start infection.

Viruses infect T-helper cells and begin to duplicate themselves.

T-helper cells are weakened and reduced in number.

Killer T cells are diminished and body is more vulnerable to all infections.

B cells are stimulated to produce antibodies against viruses.

ies that are made to fight any other virus. Because the AIDS antibodies are so unique, it is possible to test a person's blood for them. If they are present, this is *almost* definite proof that a person has been infected by the AIDS virus. (I'll explain the *almost* later.)

It takes about two weeks after infection before these antibodies begin to form, and six to eight weeks before most people have enough antibodies in their blood to make the blood test for AIDS positive. In some people, this may take as long as four to six months.

The function of these antibodies is to neutralize the virus that caused them to form, and that's what happens in most infections—but not with AIDS. In spite of the antibodies, the virus continues to grow inside the T-helper cells—damaging and destroying these vital cells and decreasing their number and strength. As this happens, the immune system is slowly weakened.

People who become infected with the AIDS virus may live the rest of their lives without any symptoms or illness, or they may develop a debilitating illness that ultimately takes their lives. For convenience, the entire range of the disease caused by the virus has been divided into four stages, which I will describe. However, there are really no clear-cut dividing lines between these stages, and for some people the course of the disease may not fit perfectly into any of the categories.

Stage 1: Acute Infection

Within three to fourteen days of the time that they become infected with the AIDS virus, a very small minority of people will develop an acute flu-like illness, with fever, swollen glands, headache, and weakness. Many will also have a peeling skin rash. These symptoms may last for two to three weeks and then subside, at which time the person enters a symptom-free stage (Stage 2). It is important to note that all of these symptoms and signs of acute AIDS infection can occur as a result of other—less serious—medical problems such as mononucleosis or allergic drug reactions. The diagnosis of AIDS or AIDS virus infection should never be made just because a person has these symptoms.

Stage 2: Silent Infection

Most people who are infected with the AIDS virus never go through the stage of acute infection. Instead, they enter a silent or "asymptomatic" stage, during which they have no symptoms at all. In some of these people, the only evidence that they have been infected is a positive blood test for antibodies against the AIDS virus. Others may show subtle signs of damage to their immune systems, but these are not severe enough to make them more susceptible to infections or other diseases.

Recent research suggests that the silent stage may last much longer than was originally believed possible. Some studies show that a person may remain in this stage for fifteen years before developing signs of real illness. Although they may feel well during the silent stage, every infected person must be considered capable of spreading the AIDS virus to others during this time. Within five years, at least 30 percent of those who become infected and enter the silent stage will go on to develop symptoms, entering the third stage of the disease. Many experts believe that—ultimately— everyone who is infected with the virus will develop the actual illness.

Stage 3: AIDS-Related Complex (ARC)

The appearance of symptoms after a silent period usually signals the stage of the disease known as AIDS-Related Complex (ARC). The most conspicuous physical change in ARC is the development of persistent swelling of the lymph glands, especially those in the back of the neck, the armpits, and the back of the mouth (the tonsils).

Other signs that the disease has progressed to this stage include persistent fever, night sweats, fatigue, peeling skin rashes, and unexplained weight loss. People with ARC may also develop diarrhea, which can cause severe weight loss and weakens them greatly. Without treatment, the ARC stage will last from a few months to years, after which the disease progresses to a final stage that can truly be called AIDS.

Stage 4: AIDS

The final stage of the disease begins when the immune system is disabled to the point that it can no longer protect the body against diseases a healthy person can resist. A person with AIDS has all of the symptoms and problems that occur with ARC, but is now also struck with life-threatening diseases. These include severe opportunistic infections, such as pneumonia or tuberculosis, that healthy people would not get (so-called because they take advantage of a lapse in the strength of the immune system). They also develop cancers like Kaposi's sarcoma that wouldn't occur if the immune system were healthy.

Even when free of opportunistic infections or cancer, the person with AIDS feels sick most of the time. Within six months, most are no longer able to work. During this stage of the illness they can expect to be in and out of the hospital, and continually taking medication for the complications that occur. In some patients with AIDS, the virus enters the brain, causing personality changes, strange behavior, and deterioration of memory and judgment.

At the present time, more than 90 percent of the people who advance to this stage of AIDS will be dead within two years.

What Triggers the Passage from Stage to Stage?

AIDS infections have been likened to forest fires in which embers can burn quietly in one spot for weeks before either burning out or erupting into flames that destroy an entire forest. So, too, the AIDS virus may smolder forever in some of its victims, while it rages out of control in the bodies of others.

In the forest, heat, wind, or low humidity cause the flames to burst forth. In the human, there appear to be comparable factors that unleash the full fury of the AIDS virus. These include:

• stimulation or suppression of the immune system,
• repeated exposure to the AIDS virus,
• genetic factors.

For reasons that are not completely understood, anything that stimulates the immune system appears to be capable of accelerating the course of AIDS.

Infections or immunizations will do this, and it is possible that an illness as common as influenza may also be able to trigger trouble.

Anything that suppresses the immune system can also cause problems, as this suppression adds to the loss of immunity that the AIDS virus has caused. The hazards are especially great for anyone taking immunosuppressive drugs to treat cancer or to prevent rejection after an organ transplant.

Repeated exposure to the AIDS virus may also accelerate the course of the disease. For this reason, two people who are both infected with the virus may worsen the course of their disease by having sex with each other.

As with many other medical problems, genetic differences probably help to explain why AIDS remains dormant in some people and progresses so rapidly in others. Although such factors would seem to be beyond a person's control, the truth is that some people are able to utilize much more of their inherited immune strength than are others because they take better care of themselves.

HOW DID THIS HAPPEN?

We are not certain exactly how or where AIDS began, but the evidence suggests that it is not a brand-new disease. Samples of blood that have been frozen for years in Africa reveal evidence of AIDS antibodies, and huge numbers of people in some African countries are infected with it now. It is likely that the disease has existed there for years, but escaped attention because of inadequate systems for treating and reporting infectious diseases.

One popular theory among AIDS experts is that an ancestor of the AIDS virus actually started in rural areas of Africa in primate animals such as monkeys, and spread to man when these animals were slaughtered for food. The urbanization of Africa would have brought infected men or women into the cities, where sexual contact would then have fueled the spread of the virus.

In an age of jet travel and free sexual life-styles, it is not difficult to imagine how one infected person from Africa could have introduced the virus into other countries and quickly have infected large numbers of people. We can credit an alert medical community and an efficient public health system in the United States for bringing this disease into the public eye at a time when relatively small numbers of Americans were actually exhibiting signs of illness.

Today, no country in the world and no sector of society can be guaranteed safe from contact with the AIDS virus. Millions of infected people are alive and seemingly well in the silent stage of the disease—virtually every one of them capable of spreading the virus to others, and many of them currently engaged in activities that will do so.

HOW CAN *AIDS* BE STOPPED?

There are three basic ways to stop the spread of any infectious disease. The best, of course, is to keep people who are not infected with the disease from coming into contact with the germ that causes it. Since that is difficult in today's busy and crowded world, two other strategies have come to play essential roles in controlling infectious disease—immunization and chemotherapy (antibiotics and antiviral drugs). Unfortunately, neither of these strategies is working against the AIDS virus.

At the present time, there are no vaccines that have been proven effective against the AIDS virus in humans, and none are likely to be widely available for years. The search for an AIDS vaccine is frustrated by the fact that the AIDS virus—like the viruses that cause the common cold—appears to have many different shapes and characteristics. A vaccine that works against one form of the virus is not necessarily going to be effective against another.

It is hoped that genetic engineering techniques will enable researchers to produce a vaccine based on an internal element that is common to all varieties of the AIDS virus. But even the most optimistic experts say that a marketable version of such a vaccine is at least five years away. The pessimistic ones predict a wait of ten years or more.

A similar problem exists in finding a drug that will cure AIDS, although there has been limited success with drugs that slow the growth of the virus. The problem lies in the fact that the genetic material of the virus literally incorporates itself into the genetic material of the cell. At present, to eliminate the virus you have to kill the cell.

One drug, Azidothymidine (also currently known as AZT, Retrovir, and zidovudine), has proven capable in some cases of preventing the virus from duplicating itself by blocking a key step in its reproductive process. But AZT has many toxic side effects and cannot be tolerated by all people with AIDS. Once use of the drug is stopped, the virus starts to duplicate itself again and the disease resumes its destructive course.

That leaves avoidance of infection as the only completely effective way of combatting AIDS today. That strategy is the subject of Chapter 3.

CHAPTER TWO

How AIDS Is Spread

THE TRANSMISSION OF THE *AIDS* VIRUS

AIDS is spread when infected fluids from one person are introduced into the body of another person. In persons known to be infected, the virus has been found in almost every body fluid that has been tested for it so far. In theory, that should mean that the disease is fairly easy to transmit from one person to another, but in actual practice, this does not appear to be the case.

The AIDS virus is a delicate organism and will not live long without the right nutrients and environmental conditions. It can be inactivated immediately with a weak solution (10 percent) of household bleach. It requires moist, warm conditions to survive.

Semen appears to be a particularly effective agent for spreading AIDS, because the virus concentrates in large numbers there. Almost two thirds of AIDS cases in the United States to date were spread by means of infected semen, according to statistics released by the Centers for Disease Control.

The great majority of these cases have involved homosexual or bisexual males, but a significant number were people who claimed to have had only heterosexual contact. Frozen semen used in artificial insemination has been proven responsible for several cases of AIDS infection. It is believed that the AIDS virus is also present in fluids discharged from the penis before actual ejaculation.

It is important to note that not every contact with infected semen results in the spread of AIDS. Studies show that some people have been able to escape infection despite contact with such semen. However, the research also shows that your risk of eventually becoming infected does go up each time you tempt fate with such contact.

It appears that the amount of virus present in a body fluid affects the ability of that fluid to infect a person. It may be that the body can fight off the small concentrations of the virus found in fluids like saliva or tears, but is unable to cope with the greater amounts present in blood or semen. Studies of dental professionals show how difficult it is to transmit the AIDS virus through saliva. Despite millions of contacts with AIDS-infected patients, none of these health workers are known to have contracted AIDS through these exposures.

Blood transmission is responsible for about 20 percent of all the AIDS cases in the United States, but transfusions account for only a small share of that number (2 or 3 percent). The sharing of contaminated needles by IV (intravenous) drug abusers has always been —and continues to be—the major factor here.

Amazingly enough, it is possible to have direct contact with infected blood without getting the infection. Large numbers of medical personnel who have accidentally stuck themselves with needles used on infected patients are grateful for that fact. In one survey that included hundreds of health workers who stuck themselves accidentally with needles used on infected patients—and who had none of the risk factors for AIDS themselves—there were only three people whose test for AIDS antibodies turned positive. The low incidence of antibodies in this group is probably due to the fact that they came in contact with infected blood only once, and then only with a tiny amount.

At one time, medical transfusions of blood and blood products were responsible for a larger share of AIDS infections. However, several measures have cut the risk of infection to extremely low levels—somewhere between 1 in 100,000 and 1 in a million transfusions. This has been accomplished by screening out people at high risk for AIDS as donors and by careful testing of every unit of blood donated.

Babies are another group that has been infected by blood transmission. This happens either during pregnancy, when the virus passes into the fetus through the placental blood flow, or at the time of delivery, when the infant comes in contact with the mother's infected blood in the birth canal. At least 50 percent of babies born to infected mothers will get AIDS. Of this group, almost all will be dead within a year.

An incident in Australia makes it clear that babies can become infected through their mothers' milk. A woman who was not infected when she delivered her baby was transfused after delivery. She nursed the child, and the baby became infected with the AIDS virus. Since the mother was infected by blood she received *after* she delivered the baby, it was concluded that the infant was infected by its mother's milk.

The AIDS virus has been demonstrated many times to exist in the cervical and vaginal fluids of women who are infected. This is believed to be the primary way in which AIDS is transmitted from women to men. Unlike fertility, there is no "safe" period with respect to transmission of the AIDS virus. It has been found to be present at every stage of the menstrual cycle and clearly appears able to spread the infection from women to men during vaginal intercourse.

In Africa, where almost as many women as men are infected with AIDS, vaginal intercourse is a very common mechanism for spreading the disease. More and more cases are being found in the United States that have been spread this way, and it is expected that this will become a common means of spread within a few years.

The AIDS virus has also been found in urine, tears, stool, and fluids taken from joints. Although there have been no documented cases of the virus being spread by contact with any of these fluids, in theory the possibility exists. It is possible, in fact, that this has already happened, but that we are simply not aware that this was the means of spread. If this is true, the number of these cases is extremely small when compared to the number spread by infected semen, blood, and vaginal fluids.

Whatever the fluid involved, it is likely that the risk of infection increases with the number of times a person is exposed to the virus. Several studies have shown that having sexual contact with many different partners will increase your risk of infection. But it also appears that repeated contact with the same infected partner will increase your chance of becoming infected.

We still don't know why some people can have repeated sexual exposure to infected fluids and *not* get infected. Learning the answer to that question could provide a major breakthrough in the fight against this disease.

HOW THE *AIDS* VIRUS IS *NOT* SPREAD

AIDS is not transmitted by casual contact. You don't pick it up from dishes, drinking glasses, or food. To prove his belief in this fact, the director of the California State Health Department took his wife and his entire office staff to dinner at a restaurant in Sacramento where the chef had died of AIDS.

In one study of hundreds of people who lived in the same household as someone with AIDS, there was no evidence that the virus could be spread by close, nonsexual contact (the contact included hugging, kissing, and sharing of kitchen and bathroom facilities). In another study of a European boarding school attended by many children who had hemophilia and AIDS virus infections, none of the healthy children in the school showed evidence of infection despite very close contact with their infected schoolmates.

Researchers also studied ninety children who lived in households with AIDS patients. At the start of the study, none of these children had antibodies to the AIDS virus and all remained free of infection at the end. Even brothers and sisters of young children with AIDS (hemophiliacs who received infected blood products) remained free of infection. These studies support the belief that the AIDS virus is not spread through close physical contact except when body fluids are exchanged.

AIDS is not spread by mosquitoes either, although some people in Belle Glade, a rural town in Florida, blamed these insects when it was discovered that there was a high incidence of AIDS within the town limits. However, when citizens of all ages were tested for evidence of AIDS antibodies, no children under the age of ten had been infected. Since mosquitoes are not known to discriminate by age, researchers were forced to conclude that the sexual activity of the older residents was responsible for the high incidence of the disease. It turned out that the vast majority of those who were infected had a history of AIDS-related behavior—they were homosexuals, drug users, or sex partners of someone in those high-risk categories.

Contrary to rumors that existed at one time, the AIDS virus is not spread by vaccines, although vaccination does challenge the immune system and could make AIDS flare up in a person who is already infected. When the vaccine contains a live virus, there is even a danger that the person will get the disease that the immunization was supposed to prevent. In one rare case, a sailor infected with AIDS developed smallpox after immunization.

CHAPTER THREE

Safe Sex

The best protection against the infection right now, barring abstinence, is the use of a condom. A condom should be used during sexual relations from start to finish with anyone whom you are not absolutely sure is free of the AIDS virus.
—Everett Koop, M.D.,
Surgeon General of the United States

Not one TV station in the nation missed that juicy quote. There he was, the Surgeon General of the United States, telling America to put on condoms. It was a condom manufacturer's dream. And for those with real concerns about getting AIDS, it was like a reprieve sent from heaven.

But there were a few things the Surgeon General forgot to mention. He left out the fact that condoms don't seem to work as well in real life as they do in the laboratory. He never pointed out that condoms are not likely to be any more effective against AIDS than they are against conception.

How effective is that? When one hundred couples use condoms correctly and consistently for contraception, the *best* they can expect is that two of the women will be pregnant at the end of a year. In actual practice, the pregnancy rate among couples who use condoms is much higher—10 percent or more per year. (To learn more about why condoms fail, see Chapter 4.)

That's not an acceptable failure rate when the price for failure is getting a disease that can kill you.

The Surgeon General had good intentions, but I'm convinced that people got the wrong impression from what he said. And he wasn't the only person in a position of authority saying such things. College students were treated to similar statements by the staffs of their campus health services, with free condoms thrown in for good measure. At Dartmouth, they were handing out kits: a "safe sex" brochure, a condom, a tube of lubricant jelly (to lessen trauma in tight places), and a rubber dam (a piece of latex used to cover the genital or anal area during oral contact).

Even Walt Disney Studios got in on the act. In an educational video designed for junior high and high school students, youngsters were told that the best they could do to protect themselves against AIDS was to "know their partner" (whatever that means to a teenager), wear a condom during intercourse, avoid anal intercourse, and not make sexual decisions while using drugs or alcohol. I'm sorry, but that's not the best they can do. The Disney folks forgot to mention abstinence, which is the only behavior that carries a 100 percent guarantee of safety.*

I think it's time to stop talking about "safe sex." I believe we should be talking about safe partners instead. A safe partner is one who has never been infected with the AIDS virus. With a safe partner, you don't have to worry about getting AIDS yourself—no matter what you do sexually, and no matter how much protection you use while you do it.

Truly "safe sex" is an all-or-nothing thing. Sex is either 100 percent safe or it's not, even when it's "almost safe." If you can't find a safe partner, don't kid yourself into believing that there is a perfectly safe alternative—other than abstinence.

But no one talks about abstinence today. Judging by

---

*In January 1987, Disney Studios modified its video for youngsters by putting the following message before the title:

Medical experts agree that the most effective way to protect oneself against the AIDS virus is to abstain from sexual intercourse and to avoid intravenous drugs.

In March, the decision was made to revise the video itself. Disney executives tell me that the narration will be rewritten to incorporate abstinence as one of the measures recommended within the body of the program itself.

my mail, it was a somewhat surprised—but approving—"Today" show audience who heard me suggest that abstinence is a reasonable alternative in these dangerous times. And I'll say it again. If you can't be sure that you've got a safe partner, abstinence is the only sexual practice you can consider safe.

I believe that complete abstention from sexual activities with others is a choice that deserves serious consideration in the age of AIDS. It's a particularly good choice for people who are carrying the AIDS virus and risk the lives of others by engaging in sexual activities with them—even with partners who are also carrying the AIDS virus. There is evidence to suggest that the chance of AIDS progressing beyond the silent stage is related to the number of times you receive additional "doses" of the virus that infected you, or a dose of a slightly different strain.

I believe that abstinence is an especially good option for the youngsters of our world. They often lack the judgment and control needed to keep themselves safe in sexually exciting situations, and they have many more years ahead of them—hopefully safer years—during which they can make up for lost time if they feel the need to.

I should make it clear that my suggestions about abstinence have nothing to do with moral issues. The only issue is survival. If you want to be certain of survival, you have only two choices: abstinence or a safe partner.

How do you find a safe partner? You may already have one. If you have had a completely monogamous relationship with a partner who has not had sex with anyone else during the past ten years—or who has not been infected through IV drug use or blood transfusions—you already have a safe partner, and *anything* you do with that partner is safe as far as AIDS is concerned.

Even if your partner has had sex with someone else, he or she *may* be safe. It all depends on whether or not that "someone else" carried the AIDS virus, and whether or not your partner picked it up.

More and more people are beginning to question their partners about their past sexual history. It's difficult, and it can be embarrassing, but—considering the stakes—it seems like a worthwhile thing to do. The more you know about your partner's sexual history, the better you can estimate the likelihood that he or she is free of the AIDS virus.

It's important to remember that what you learn only allows you to *estimate* your partner's safety, because you are relying completely on your partner's honesty and, in some cases, his or her estimate of *other* partners' safety. To my mind, that's a really big weakness because many people find it difficult to be candid about their sexual adventures (especially their misadventures). But it's better than not asking at all.

Because of this weakness, you should not rely completely on this technique in deciding that your partner is safe. Use it instead as a screening technique—to identify high-risk partners who are decent enough to answer you honestly, and to identify those whose responses are suspicious enough to warrant caution on your part.

Here are the questions you should ask to help determine just how risky your partner is for the AIDS virus. I'll show you how to score the answers at the end of the list.

1. Do you have AIDS or an illness like AIDS?
2. Have you ever had a positive test result on a test for antibodies against the AIDS virus?
3. Are you bisexual (ask of men) or are any of your sex partners bisexual (ask of women)?
4. Have you ever used illegal drugs (some people call them "recreational" drugs) intravenously?
5. Have you had sex with a prostitute in the last ten years?
6. Have you had more than one sex partner in the last ten years? (The greater the number, the greater the risk that one of them was carrying the AIDS virus.)
7. Did any of your sex partners use IV drugs?
8. Did any of your sex partners come from countries where the incidence of AIDS is extremely high (some African countries and Haiti)?
9. Have you ever been rejected from donating blood in the last ten years and, if so, why? (Among the rea-

sons for rejection of blood donations are positive tests for the AIDS virus and other sexually transmitted diseases. People who had positive tests for any disease that could be transmitted sexually are statistically at high risk for also carrying the AIDS virus.)

A "yes" answer to any question on this list indicates an increased risk of AIDS infection. The lower on the list a question falls, the less risk a "yes" answer to it implies.

The most accurate way to tell if your partner is "safe" is by having him or her get a blood test for AIDS antibodies. Even that test leaves some room for error, but—together with a good history—it's the most accurate way to find a safe partner. We'll show you how to do that in the next chapter. At the same time, you'll find out how to tell if you are a safe partner yourself.

CHAPTER FOUR

Almost Safe Sex

al·most ('ol mōst) *adv* slightly short of; not quite; all but; very nearly.

If a safe partner is not a possible alternative for you, and abstinence is not an acceptable choice, you still don't have to resort to a high-risk alternative. There are many ways to decrease your chances of coming in contact with the AIDS virus while still remaining reasonably active sexually.

There are three things you can do to lower your risk of infection with AIDS:

- pick safer partners,
- use safer practices,
- use protective devices.

Each of these strategies will reduce your likelihood of coming into contact with the AIDS virus. I can't tell you exactly what your risk will be, but one thing is certain with this approach: it does not come down to zero. You should try to get it as close to zero as you can, and keep it there.

Even if you have already taken some risks that you wish you hadn't, it's not too late to begin to protect yourself. Research suggests that the chance of being infected during a single encounter with an infected partner is actually low. If you've made it through that encounter without picking up the virus, you get to start all over again with a clean slate.

So don't continue with high-risk behavior just because you did it in the past. That advice may seem obvious, but it's worth emphasizing because some people assume that they've got nothing more to lose after having had sex with someone who's carrying the AIDS virus. Nothing could be further from the truth.

PICKING SAFER PARTNERS

Which Partner Would You Pick?

Assume for a moment that you live in a small city in North Dakota (an obviously low-risk state for AIDS because only four cases have ever been reported there). Which of the following sex partners would you

AIDS CASES BY TRANSMISSION CATEGORIES*

Transmission Categories	Males Number	(%)	Females Number	(%)	Total Number	(%)
Homosexual/ Bisexual Male	21,279	(71)			21,279	(66)
Intravenous (IV) Drug Abuser	4,296	(14)	1,125	(51)	5,421	(17)
Homosexual Male and IV Drug Abuser	2,502	(8)			2,502	(8)
Hemophilia/ Coagulation Disorder	267	(1)	7	(0)	274	(1)
Heterosexual Cases	613	(2)	608	(28)	1,221	(4)
Transfusion, Blood or Blood Components	404	(1)	222	(10)	626	(2)
Undetermined	799	(3)	243	(11)	1,042	(3)
	30,160	(93)	2,205	(7)	32,365	(100)

choose if you were looking for one who had a low risk of carrying the virus? For simplicity, we've made each of these potential partners a man. If you are a man yourself, you can change the sex and adjust the stories so that they work for you.

*AIDS Weekly Surveillance Report, Centers for Disease Control, March 16, 1987.

Partner #1: This person is a heterosexual who has had intercourse with only one other person in his life—someone he met two years ago at a bar in your hometown.

Partner #2: This person has had sexual intercourse with only one other person in his life—a secretary in New York whom he met in the course of a business trip five years ago. His relationship with this woman (who works for his best customer) is "still good" after five years.

Partner #3: This person is a heterosexual who has had sex with six women during the last ten years. Each of those women was a fellow employee at the plant where he works and each relationship lasted for a year or more.

It looks easy, doesn't it? The smart move is to pick someone whose sexual experience is limited to your hometown and to only one partner. But life is never that simple. Let me tell you a little more about the people with whom your potential partners have had sex.

Partner #1 had never seen his young lady friend before he met her in the bar, and he has not seen her since. That's because she was a prostitute from New York heading for the warmer streets of California. She has slept with literally thousands of men and, although she never used IV drugs herself, she slept with a pimp who did.

Partner #2 thinks he's in love with the secretary in New York. That's why he has remained faithful to her for the last five years. If only the feeling were mutual. His friend is very active sexually in the weeks between his visits to New York. She has had intercourse with dozens of men during the last five years, including at least one bisexual executive from San Francisco.

Partner #3 has slept with more women than the others, but there's a difference about the women he picks. Each one was a virgin when he slept with her for the first time. In fact, that's what made them attractive to him. Little did he know how important that fact would later become to his health.

In the age of AIDS, you are no longer sleeping with just your partner. If any exchange of body fluids takes place, you are sleeping with your partner's partners, and all the accumulated risk of their sexual histories too. To the extent that you are able to limit your exposure to those with a very low risk of having an AIDS infection, you will also be limiting your own risk of becoming infected.

By studying the blood of various groups of people, researchers have been able to identify some groups whose members are much more likely to be infected with the AIDS virus. By avoiding anyone in these groups (listed from highest to lowest risk) you will significantly decrease your chance of coming in contact with the virus:

- homosexual male prostitutes,
- homosexual males who have not been involved in completely monogamous relationships and bisexual males,
- IV (intravenous) drug users,
- female prostitutes,
- heterosexual men or women with multiple sex partners,
- men or women who have had other sexually transmitted diseases.

Homosexual Male Prostitutes

The highest risk is probably found in this group, most of whom are likely to be infected with the AIDS virus. It's not surprising. Some of these men have had sexual contact with literally thousands of other men. The AIDS epidemic has dramatically reduced the frequency of sexual contacts by male prostitutes—by killing some and frightening many others. But the streets of my city are still dotted with these people—men whose self-esteem and self-control is so low that they continue their suicidal and homicidal activities in spite of the terrifying risks.

One can only assume that these men believe they

have little left to lose themselves. They are high-risk takers who care little about the personal consequences of their behavior, and who probably have no concern about the effects of their behavior on others. Some of these men are driven by sexual compulsions that make it impossible for them to control their behavior.

Homosexual Males Who Have Not Been Involved in Completely Monogamous Relationships and Bisexual Males

An extremely high proportion of this group has been shown to be positive for AIDS antibodies and must be assumed capable of transmitting the virus to others through sexual contact. Even those men whose sexual activity has been limited to a small number of partners are at great risk of carrying the virus because one or more of their partners may have been among those who have had sex with huge numbers of others.

The risk that a homosexual or bisexual male is infected with the AIDS virus is also dependent on the cities in which he has been sexually active. In San Francisco, seven out of ten homosexual and bisexual males have antibodies against the AIDS virus, while in Long Beach, California, only 30 percent of the men in this group are infected. It seems reasonable that the incidence of infection would be much lower in those cities and states where AIDS is almost nonexistent. But don't forget—it takes only one trip to San Francisco or New York to pick up the infection, and it takes only one infected and sexually active male to infect an entire community that was previously free of the virus.

It also takes only one bisexual man to introduce the AIDS virus into the heterosexual community. Bisexual men have a very high risk of being infected with the AIDS virus. However, the risk is easily hidden when they are having sex with women, unless they are asked about their prior sexual activities or they choose to reveal them voluntarily.

A phone survey in San Francisco showed a steady change in sexual behavior among homosexual and bisexual men between August 1984 and April 1985. The proportion of men who reported that they were monogamous, celibate, or performed "unsafe" sexual practices only with their steady partner increased from 69 percent to 81 percent.

The good news is that these changes in behavior are having an effect on the rate at which high-risk men in San Francisco are becoming infected with AIDS. Several years ago, 15 to 20 percent of the men who were negative for AIDS antibodies were turning positive each year. Today, that number is down to around 3 or 4 percent.

Other studies show that most of the men who are now turning positive are those who persist in having anal sex. Among those men who have changed to oral or manual techniques for sexual stimulation, few who started out testing negative for AIDS are turning positive.

It is important to note that men who have been involved in completely monogamous homosexual relationships for long periods of time are at much lower risk for the AIDS virus. Any such man whose relationship has existed for ten years or more should have no risk at all.

IV (Intravenous) Drug Users

An extremely high percentage of IV drug abusers—both men and women—are infected with the AIDS virus. Primarily, they have been infected by the common practice of sharing needles, a practice which moves infected blood from one person to another very effectively. Also, many men and women in this group are known to engage in prostitution to support their drug habits, which places them in those high-risk groups as well.

Female Prostitutes

The percentage of AIDS-positive women in this group is very high, in part because of the large number of men with whom they have contact and in part because of the life-styles of their contacts. These women also may be more likely to become infected when they come in contact with the virus because their vaginal and cervical tissues may be inflamed and, therefore, more susceptible to passage of the virus into the bloodstream. Yet another risk is added by the fact that many of these women are IV drug users and/or have frequent contact with them.

As with all groups, geography has a very definite impact on the risk of AIDS infection. In March 1987, the Centers for Disease Control reported the statistics for female prostitutes (shown in the table).

AIDS ANTIBODIES IN FEMALE PROSTITUTES

Region	# of Women Tested	# of Women Positive	Percent Positive
Eastern U.S.			
Atlanta	92	1	1
Miami	252	47	19
Newark, Jersey City, Paterson	56	32	57
Western U.S.			
Colorado Springs	71	1	1
Las Vegas	34	0	0
Los Angeles	184	8	4
San Francisco	146	9	6

Heterosexual Men or Women with Multiple Sex Partners

In this case, it's just a numbers game. The more sex partners you have, the better the odds are that one of them has come in contact with the AIDS virus. The interesting thing is that your partners don't have to be promiscuous themselves to pick up the virus. As you've already learned from our "pick a partner" game, all it takes is one promiscuous partner in a sexual chain to increase the risk for the entire group. The members of two "swinging" social/sexual groups in Minnesota learned this lesson the hard way when one woman in each of the groups tested positive for AIDS antibodies. Because of the extraordinary amount of sexual communication between the members of these groups, hundreds of active heterosexuals in Minnesota must now live in fear that they, too, have been infected.

Men or Women Who Have Had Other Sexually Transmitted Diseases

Men or women who have had any sexually transmitted diseases (including sexually transmitted Hepatitis-B, a

EFFECT OF AIDS INFORMATION ON NUMBER OF SEXUAL PARTNERS

	Average Number of Partners in Past Six Months	
	Before Learning About AIDS	After Learning About AIDS
Male homosexuals and bisexuals	5.3	3.2
Male heterosexuals	2.2	1.8
Female heterosexuals	1.9	1.8

disease that can be transmitted by other means as well) statistically have a much higher risk of also having other sexually transmitted diseases, and should be considered at high risk of carrying the AIDS virus. These people may be much more willing to admit that they have had such "lesser" problems, and that clue can be helpful in guiding you away from high-risk partners.

The information about AIDS is finally beginning to sink in and people are decreasing the number of partners with whom they have sex. This should slow the spread of AIDS. In San Francisco, a 1986 study of single men showed that the average number of sexual partners each man had was dropping steadily. The results are summarized in the preceding table.

So it's all a question of risks and benefits. Some places are more risky than others. Some people are more risky than others. Some practices are more risky than others. The goal of this book is to help you understand those risks and—I hope—to motivate you to keep yours low.

GEOGRAPHY AND *AIDS* RISK

One way to find safer partners—though a bit impractical for most—is to move to a place where the incidence of AIDS is low. There are two states that have reported only four cases of AIDS since the disease was discovered, while others are crowded with AIDS patients. Although this near-freedom from AIDS cannot be expected to last forever, the relative differences between states like Nebraska and New York are likely to last.

Although no city is immune from AIDS, some cities have a much higher incidence of the disease than others. In these high-risk cities, research shows that a much higher proportion of the supposedly "well" population tests positive for antibodies to the AIDS virus. (See tables.)

AIDS CASES BY STATE OF RESIDENCE*

State of Residence	Year Ending March 16, 1987		Cumulative Total Since June 1981	
	Number	Percent	Number	Percent
New York	3986	(27.5)	10091	(30.7)
California	3286	(22.7)	7486	(22.8)
Florida	976	(6.7)	2199	(6.7)

AIDS CASES BY STATE OF RESIDENCE*

State of Residence	Year Ending March 16, 1987		Cumulative Total Since June 1981	
	Number	Percent	Number	Percent
Texas	1049	(7.2)	2056	(6.3)
New Jersey	793	(5.5)	1894	(5.8)
Illinois	374	(2.6)	770	(2.3)
Pennsylvania	296	(2.0)	708	(2.2)
Massachusetts	315	(2.2)	678	(2.1)
Georgia	350	(2.4)	656	(2.0)
District of Columbia	248	(1.7)	586	(1.8)
Maryland	246	(1.7)	509	(1.6)
Washington	197	(1.4)	402	(1.2)
Louisiana	189	(1.3)	395	(1.2)
Connecticut	185	(1.3)	391	(1.2)
Virginia	146	(1.0)	363	(1.1)
Colorado	176	(1.2)	338	(1.0)
Puerto Rico	113	(0.8)	324	(1.0)
Ohio	179	(1.2)	302	(0.9)
Michigan	160	(1.1)	293	(0.9)
Missouri	107	(0.7)	203	(0.6)
North Carolina	91	(0.6)	199	(0.6)
Arizona	77	(0.5)	174	(0.5)
Minnesota	87	(0.6)	172	(0.5)
Indiana	74	(0.5)	146	(0.4)
Oregon	61	(0.4)	127	(0.4)
Hawaii	61	(0.4)	117	(0.4)
South Carolina	44	(0.3)	114	(0.3)
Tennessee	62	(0.4)	101	(0.3)
Wisconsin	59	(0.4)	100	(0.3)
Oklahoma	64	(0.4)	99	(0.3)
Nevada	46	(0.3)	78	(0.2)
Alabama	30	(0.2)	75	(0.2)
Kentucky	29	(0.2)	67	(0.2)
Kansas	44	(0.3)	65	(0.2)
Rhode Island	37	(0.3)	63	(0.2)

AIDS CASES BY STATE OF RESIDENCE*

State of Residence	Year Ending March 16, 1987		Cumulative Total Since June 1981	
	Number	Percent	Number	Percent
Utah	25	(0.2)	59	(0.2)
New Mexico	31	(0.2)	53	(0.2)
Arkansas	32	(0.2)	51	(0.2)
Delaware	24	(0.2)	48	(0.1)
Mississippi	28	(0.2)	44	(0.1)
Iowa	20	(0.1)	40	(0.1)
Maine	22	(0.2)	39	(0.1)
New Hampshire	18	(0.1)	28	(0.1)
Alaska	10	(0.1)	25	(0.1)
Nebraska	12	(0.1)	25	(0.1)
West Virginia	9	(0.1)	22	(0.1)
Vermont	5	(0.0)	11	(0.0)
Idaho	4	(0.0)	8	(0.0)
Montana	6	(0.0)	7	(0.0)
Virgin Islands	3	(0.0)	7	(0.0)
Wyoming	4	(0.0)	7	(0.0)
North Dakota	1	(0.0)	4	(0.0)
South Dakota	2	(0.0)	4	(0.0)
Guam			1	(0.0)
Trust Territory			1	(0.0)
Total	14,493	(100.0)	32,825	(100.0)

This has occurred, in part, because the percentage of homosexual men in the population is much larger in some cities than in others. San Francisco, for example, with its tolerant attitude toward alternative life-

*AIDS Weekly Surveillance Report, Centers for Disease Control, March 16, 1987.

styles, has long attracted many homosexual men from other parts of the country. Tragically, the concentration of so many homosexual men in one area has

AIDS CASES BY STANDARD METROPOLITAN STATISTICAL AREA (SMSA) OF RESIDENCE*

SMSA of Residence	Population (in Millions)	Number of AIDS Cases	Number of AIDS Cases per Million Population
New York, NY	9.12	9,191	1,007
San Francisco, CA	3.25	3,315	1,020
Los Angeles, CA	7.48	2,811	375
Houston, TX	2.91	1,036	356
Miami, FL	1.63	977	599
Washington, DC	3.06	925	302
Newark, NJ	1.97	775	393
Chicago, IL	7.10	682	96
Dallas, TX	2.97	588	197
Philadelphia, PA	4.72	578	122
Atlanta, GA	2.03	511	252
Boston, MA	2.76	498	180
Nassau-Suffolk, NY	2.61	387	148
Ft. Lauderdale, FL	1.02	380	373
San Diego, CA	1.86	377	203
Jersey City, NJ	0.56	351	626
Seattle, WA	1.61	315	195
REST OF U.S.	173.47	9,128	53
Total	230.11	32,825	143

*AIDS Weekly Surveillance Report, Centers for Disease Control, March 16, 1987.

facilitated the spread of the AIDS virus in several large cities.

New York, Newark, and Miami are also high-risk areas because of the prevalence of IV drug abuse. Sexual activity—especially prostitution—has helped spread the AIDS virus out of the drug-using group and into the surrounding general population.

It stands to reason, therefore, that a sexually active person in a high-risk city is more likely to have come in contact with the AIDS virus than someone in a low-risk city, even if the number of different sex partners they have had is the same. And it is likely that the AIDS virus has not yet reached some areas of the country, so even the most promiscuous activities in these areas are—for the moment—free of risk.

Although it is reasonable to assume that some cities and states will always have a higher risk than others because of their large homosexual populations or their problems with drug abuse, it will not be long before no area can be considered "geographically" safe from AIDS. Between 1 and 2 million people are believed to be carrying the AIDS virus, and their travels have taken them far and wide. Every community in the country whose citizens have traveled beyond the city limits, and every community that has allowed travelers inside, must assume that the AIDS virus is present now, or soon will be.

SAFER SEXUAL PRACTICES

Research studies confirm the notion that some sexual practices are safer than others with respect to their likelihood of transmitting AIDS viruses. This has led some people to classify different sexual practices in groups ranging from "safe" to "dangerous."

By themselves, these classifications are extremely misleading because they ignore the issue of whether your partner is carrying the AIDS virus. The truth is, if your partner is free of the virus, there is no sexual act you can perform with this partner that will give you AIDS. And if your partner is carrying the virus, there are few things you can do—other than cuddling—that any thinking human being would call 100 percent safe.

In the material that follows, you'll find the best estimation we can make as to the relative safety of common sexual practices. Keep in mind that these are estimates only, and they apply only to large groups of people. In any given person, a unique factor might reverse the odds completely.

For example, the list you are about to read says that anal-receptive sex is much more dangerous than anal-insertive. The reverse might be true if the insertive partner has a sore or broken skin on or near the penis, making it easier for the virus to enter his body.

Here's our best estimate of the risks to you for different sexual practices if your partner is infected with the virus, starting with the most risky:

- anal-receptive intercourse,
- vaginal-receptive intercourse,
- anal-insertive intercourse,
- vaginal-insertive intercourse,
- oral-anal stimulation,
- oral-genital stimulation.

Anal-Receptive Intercourse
(This means that your partner's penis is inserted into your rectum.)

Several studies demonstrate that this is the sexual activity most likely to introduce the AIDS virus into your body. Though we are not sure exactly why this is true, there are several plausible explanations:

- There are many blood vessels in the anus and rectum, so the virus can get into your bloodstream more easily if it is deposited in that area.
- The AIDS virus is contained in large amounts in semen. There is good reason to believe that the more virus that is present when you are exposed, the more likely you are to become infected.
- Anal intercourse often results in tiny tears of the tissues lining the anus and rectum, which are drier and

less elastic than, for instance, vaginal tissues. This literally opens the door for entry of the virus into your bloodstream.

- The cells of the rectum may be receptive to direct infection by the AIDS virus, unlike many other cells of the body. This would enable the virus to gain a "foothold" in your body, from which the virus could be spread to other cells and other organs.

Vaginal-Receptive Intercourse

(This refers to the sexual activity of a *woman* when her male partner inserts his penis into her vagina.)

For many of the same reasons that anal-receptive sex is particularly unsafe, vaginal-receptive sex also appears to be a high-risk activity. There is strong evidence that the AIDS virus can be spread from men to women in this way. Several factors can influence the ease of spread, including the following:

- The presence of an open sore on the vagina, cervix, or external genitals: this eliminates the protective effect of the normal vaginal tissues and creates more direct access for the AIDS virus into the bloodstream.
- The presence of inflammation on the cervix or in the vaginal tissues: this increases the amount of blood flow in this area, which facilitates entry of

the virus. It also causes an increased number of white blood cells in the area where semen is deposited. Since white blood cells are the natural target of the AIDS virus, this may increase the risk significantly.

Anal-Insertive Intercourse
(This means that you insert your penis into the rectum of your male or female partner.)

Research shows that the risk of AIDS infection is much less for the insertive partner during anal sex than for the receptive partner. In one study, the incidence of AIDS was 2 to 3 percent in homosexual men who played only the insertive role, as opposed to 50 to 60 percent in those who were receptive partners.

The difference probably occurs because the receptive partner is left with large amounts of virus in the deposited semen that remain in contact with the rectal lining for long periods of time. Although the AIDS virus has been shown to be present in the stool of infected people, the insertive partner is likely to contact less virus and for shorter periods of time.

Among the factors that could increase the risk for the insertive partner are the following:

- sores or skin breaks on the penis that make it easier for the virus, if present, to enter the bloodstream,

- injury to the receptive partner that causes bleeding and increases the opportunity for exposure to the virus.

Vaginal-Insertive Intercourse
(This refers to the sexual activity of a *man* when he inserts his penis into the vagina of his female partner.)

Though it was once believed that infected women could not pass the AIDS virus to men through sexual activities, several studies have shown that this is definitely possible and may, in time, become a major source of spread in the heterosexual community.

In women who are infected with the AIDS virus, large concentrations of the virus can be found in secretions from the cervix and in vaginal fluids. During vaginal intercourse, the virus comes in contact with the urethral opening at the end of the penis. Though this area is quite small, it appears to be very susceptible with respect to transmission of the virus from a woman to a man, particularly if there is inflammation within the urethra.

It is important to note that there is no "safe" period during which the AIDS virus is absent, unlike the "safe" period that occurs with respect to fertility. The virus has been cultured at all stages of the menstrual cycle, including during the menstrual period itself.

Several factors could increase the risk of AIDS virus transmission from the female to the male during vaginal intercourse, including:

- the presence of a sore on the penis or any break in the skin,
- trauma to the vagina during intercourse that resulted in bleeding by the woman.

Oral-Anal Stimulation
(This involves the use of one partner's tongue to stimulate the anal area of the other partner, whether or not the tongue actually enters the anus.)

Though this technique is much less likely to spread the AIDS virus than the others listed above, there is evidence that it can happen. The virus has been isolated from both saliva and stool, so there is no question that exposure takes place during this kind of activity.

It is possible that this type of activity is less likely to result in transmission of the virus to the "oral" partner because of local protective factors that exist in the mouth. For reasons that are not yet completely clear, the tissues that line the mouth appear to be more resistant than other tissues. It is important to note that other serious diseases can be spread by oral-anal sex. Hepatitis viruses are commonly spread in this way.

Oral-Genital Stimulation
(This involves the stimulation of one person's genitals by the other person's mouth.)

It is believed that this form of activity spreads the AIDS virus primarily by exposing the mouth of an uninfected person to the infected semen or vaginal fluids of someone carrying the virus. In this case, it is assumed that the large amounts of virus present in genital secretions promote the spread in that direction. This practice is not necessarily made safer by having the insertive partner withdraw his penis from the mouth before ejaculation occurs, since the virus is present in pre-ejaculate fluids as well.

At least in theory, it is possible to spread the virus in the other direction, by introducing infected saliva into the vagina or urethra of an uninfected person. This may occur less often, since the amount of virus in saliva is very small.

It appears that this kind of body fluid transfer is less dangerous than that which occurs during anal sex because the lining of the mouth and vagina are more resistant to infection. Other local factors, and the fact that only small amounts of virus are present in saliva, may have something to do with it, but these are not clearly understood at this time.

THE USE OF PROTECTIVE DEVICES

Much attention has been focused on the possible role that condoms and spermicides could play in stopping the spread of AIDS. Laboratory tests have demonstrated that the AIDS virus will not penetrate the walls of an intact latex condom, and there is evidence that the AIDS virus cannot survive long periods of contact with the chemicals found in most spermicides.

There is no question that these devices—properly used—will lower the risk of infection with the AIDS virus, and I would urge their use whenever there is any possibility that one partner is infected with the virus. But I am concerned about the erroneous beliefs that many people have about condoms and spermicides— beliefs that lead them to conclude, mistakenly, that these devices offer *complete* protection during sexual activity with an infected partner. These devices will make sex *safer,* but you should not fool yourself into thinking that they make sex 100 percent safe if you or your partner is carrying the AIDS virus. If one hundred couples use condoms correctly and consistently for one year, the best they can expect is that two of the women will be pregnant at the end of the year. In actual practice, more than ten women are likely to be pregnant. Condoms fail for several reasons:

- They are not used when they should be (people are only human).
- They are used too late or they are put on incorrectly.
- They slip off (usually because they are put on the wrong way or are left on too long).
- They are defective and they tear or break (this is probably the least common reason for failure).

It is unrealistic to expect that condoms will be any more effective at preventing the spread of AIDS than they are in preventing conception, yet many people assume that the use of condoms will provide 100 percent protection.

Spermicides

The use of spermicides is also being suggested as a way to make sex safe, but there the actual picture is even less promising. Although spermicides contain a chemical called nonoxynyl-9, which has been shown to inactivate the AIDS virus in laboratory tests, there is absolutely no evidence that it is effective against the AIDS virus when human beings use it during sexual activity.

It is certainly not reasonable to expect spermicides to be more effective against the AIDS virus than they are at preventing conception, where their track record is even worse than condoms. If one hundred couples use a spermicide correctly and consistently for one year, the best they can expect is that four of the women will be pregnant at the end of the year. In actual practice, more than fifteen women are likely to be pregnant.

The combination of spermicides and condoms is believed to be more effective at preventing *conception* than either used alone. Because of this, some people are suggesting that the combination should be used to prevent AIDS also. There has been no research to prove whether this is an effective method or not. At the present time, the best recommendation appears to be to use the spermicide vaginally *in addition to a latex (not natural) condom* as a preventive measure against the AIDS virus, or if contraception is desired. (*Note:* Spermicide should not be used *inside* the condom, as it will make it much easier for the condom to slip off during intercourse. This defeats the entire purpose of using a condom.)

PUTTING IT ALL TOGETHER

There is no way to assign a precise numerical risk to any individual sexual partner or to any particular sexual practice. Though we have attempted to rank these

risks in this book, in real life there are exceptions—
"high risk" people who are *not* infected and "low risk"
people who *are*.

ESTIMATING A SEX PARTNER'S RISK FOR AIDS

	No Risk	*Low Risk*	*High Risk*
Number of sexual partners	None, or one with mutual monogamy for last ten years	Few sexual partners	Many sexual partners
Sexual preference of partners		Heterosexuals or homosexual females	Homosexual or bisexual males
Use of barrier contraceptives with others		Always used condoms	Rarely or never used condoms
Sexual practices			Played anal-receptive role
AIDS antibody test results	Negative and no sexual exposure for past six months	Negative and no sexual exposure for past three months	Positive or untested

ESTIMATING A SEX PARTNER'S RISK FOR AIDS

	No Risk	*Low Risk*	*High Risk*
Prior history of sexually transmitted disease	No	No	Yes
Use of drugs	No drug use by subject or partners	No IV drug use by subject or partners	Uses IV drugs, or sex partner uses them
Transfusions since 1978 and prior to 1985	None, or has been tested and found negative for AIDS antibodies	Transfused but not tested	Transfused many times or with large volume of blood; not tested
Places of residence		Low-incidence area for AIDS	High-incidence area for AIDS

Still, for people who are sexually active in this age of AIDS, I believe the prudent course is to keep the odds in your favor. To some extent, this table will help you do that by showing you where your sexual partners (past, present, and future) fall on the risk scale.

Don't forget that these classifications apply only to *sexual* activities; they have no bearing on nonsexual relationships. They should not be used to rationalize social avoidance or discrimination of any sort. We must not allow our concern about the sexual spread of AIDS to lead us to other inappropriate behaviors.

And don't forget the importance of acting appropriately yourself when sexually active. Use condoms if you cannot be 100 percent certain that your sexual partner is free of the virus, and avoid those practices that increase the risk of AIDS—for either of you. The small sacrifices that must be made in the name of safety are far outweighed by the potential benefits.

CHAPTER FIVE

Testing for AIDS

The screening test for AIDS is designed to detect the antibodies that are formed by the immune system after the body is infected by the AIDS virus. Though the test does not actually detect the virus itself, the presence of antibodies is an almost certain sign that an infection has taken place. (We say "almost" because the test is not perfect. It will label an *un*infected person positive for the AIDS antibody about twice in every 1,000 tests performed.)

WHO NEED NOT BE TESTED

With concern about AIDS bordering on hysteria in some quarters, the interest in AIDS testing is extremely high. However, for many people the test is not necessary and need not be done. This includes those who have been celibate or in completely monogamous relationships for ten years or more (provided they have not had blood transfusions or used IV drugs and shared needles).

WHO SHOULD BE TESTED

There are some people who believe that no one should volunteer for AIDS testing, since there is no cure for this disease. Others oppose testing because they are concerned that the results of the tests will not be kept confidential. I believe that these people—though well-intentioned—are wrong.

In the first place, if you've engaged in risky practices but have escaped infection, nothing will make you feel better now than learning that your test for AIDS is negative. I've seen many people, torn by anxiety for months, who finally broke down and had themselves tested, only to find out that all of their worry had been for naught.

If there's a chance that your test for AIDS could be positive, it is even more important that you know it. The test result warns you to guard your health more carefully, building all the resistance you can against the virus. You can also take steps to protect the health of others—by advising your past sexual partners and properly informing any potential ones.

Frankly, I believe that the time is near when we will all want to be tested—when the death toll reaches into the hundreds of thousands. Testing may even become mandatory when the need to protect society as a whole begins to outweigh the concern for individual rights.

At this time, AIDS testing is appropriate for all people who are realistically concerned that they may have come in contact with the AIDS virus. That concern is realistic if *any* of the following statements are true of you:

- You are male and have had sex with a man in the last ten years.
- You use intravenous drugs and have shared hypodermic needles, or you have had sex with someone who has done so.
- You have had sex with prostitutes in the last ten years.
- You are female and have had sex with a bisexual male.
- You have had sex with someone from a country where AIDS is epidemic.
- You have indulged in behaviors that put people at increased risk for becoming infected with the AIDS virus, and you are concerned about your status.
- You have received transfusions of blood or clotting factors between 1978 and the spring of 1985 (espe-

cially if you received large amounts of blood or the transfusions took place in a city where the incidence of AIDS is high).
- You are a health worker with a major exposure to blood from an AIDS patient.

The Surgeon General has recommended that any woman thinking of becoming pregnant should also consider being tested for AIDS antibodies, regardless of her prior sexual history. I believe that this is a reasonable precaution.

HOW THE TEST IS DONE

The first test performed is called the Enzyme-Linked Immunosorbent Assay, or ELISA, test. A half-ounce sample of blood is removed from a vein and is tested in a laboratory to see if antibodies to the AIDS virus are present.

IF YOUR *ELISA* TEST IS NEGATIVE

A negative test *should* mean that you have no antibodies against the AIDS virus and are not infected. However, it is possible to have a "false negative" result for several reasons:

- The sensitivity of the test being used was too low. The term "sensitivity" refers to the ability of the test to recognize a person infected with the AIDS virus. There are several brands of the ELISA test, each made by a different company. The sensitivity of most brands is greater than 98 percent (which means that if one hundred infected people are tested, two of them will be *erroneously* told that they are not infected).
- A mistake was made by the laboratory.
- The test was performed too soon after your contact with the virus. (If that contact was less than six months earlier, the test should be repeated after six months have passed.)
- Your body failed to make antibodies against the virus even though the infection occurred. (If this happens at all, it is very rare.)

IF YOUR *ELISA* TEST IS POSITIVE

If your ELISA test is positive, more testing must be done before any conclusion can be drawn because the ELISA test has a "false positive" rate of about 2 per 1,000. (In other words, if 1,000 uninfected people are given this test, 2 of them will be *erroneously* told that they are infected if only the results of this test are used.)

The ELISA test is extremely sensitive because it was designed, in part, to protect our supply of blood for transfusions. Unfortunately, the test is *so* sensitive that it occasionally reports an infection when none is present.

When the initial ELISA test is positive, several steps should be taken to determine the accuracy of the result. First, the original specimen should be tested again. If the result is still positive, another, more specific test—for example, the Western Blot test—should be performed. If the Western Blot test is positive, the diagnosis of infection with the AIDS virus is confirmed *for that specimen of blood.*

Before accepting that diagnosis, I would ask that a second specimen of blood—taken at a different time— be tested. This will eliminate the possibility that your first specimen was mislabeled, or that some other human error caused you to get the result of someone else's test. If a second specimen of your blood is positive on both the ELISA and a confirmatory test, the diagnosis is *confirmed* that you have been infected with the AIDS virus.

WHAT THE TEST *WON'T* TELL YOU

The ELISA and Western Blot tests will only indicate whether or not antibodies to the AIDS virus are present. There are many questions these tests cannot answer. They will not tell you when you got your infection, or from whom. They cannot tell you what your chances are of ultimately developing AIDS itself. Though these are important questions, these tests will not answer them.

WHERE TO GET TESTED

Tests for AIDS are now available everywhere—through doctors' offices, public health departments, hospital and community laboratories, and, in some larger cities, in special AIDS testing centers. A mail-order laboratory is even soliciting clients (you have to have your blood drawn somewhere in your community and send the specimen to the lab by mail).

Although the test kits used are pretty much the same from one test laboratory to the next, the attention given to processing the tests can be quite different. Your major concern when having an AIDS test should be for the accuracy of the result, so you must be careful in picking the lab that will process your test. An erroneous report could have disastrous consequences. For this reason, I advise against mail-order testing—where you have no way to confirm the quality of the work—and favor local laboratories, because participation and supervision by health professionals in your community ensures a reasonable degree of quality control. If you are not sure of where to go for a test, ask your physician for advice, call your local health department, or contact one of the referral services listed in the Counseling and Support Services section of this book.

No matter where you are tested, you should first receive counseling about the test and what the results mean (as noted earlier, different types of test kits have different levels of accuracy). You should be assured that only you, or someone you designate, will be given the results of the test, and you should be offered follow-up counseling if your test is positive.

In my opinion, the best person to go to is your own physician. This is the person who knows you best medically and can best help you interpret the results of your test. However, some people feel very uncomfortable about going to their doctor for AIDS testing because of embarrassment or out of concern for the confidentiality of the result. When you go to your doctor for an AIDS test, the result of that test becomes a part of your medical record at the doctor's office. That could make it available to others under certain circumstances (for example, if you apply for insurance, or if your medical records are subpoenaed for a lawsuit).

Almost all laboratories across the country are capable of performing the test for AIDS antibodies. Most private community laboratories and hospital laboratories will require a referral from a doctor (any doctor, not necessarily your personal physician). Most public laboratories, health departments, and free clinics will accept you for testing without such a referral. In general, all of these facilities will handle your request for testing professionally and will treat you with dignity.

In a few large cities, it is now possible to be tested for AIDS on a completely anonymous basis. In these clinics or test sites, you are identified only by number —though you must appear personally. That number is attached to the blood specimen taken from your vein, and that is the only way it can be identified in the future. At an appointed time, you call the laboratory by phone, give the technician your number, and he or she gives you the result that matches that number.

The purpose of anonymous testing is to protect you from the potential harm you might suffer if it became publicly known that you had a positive test for AIDS antibodies. Experience has already demonstrated that leakage of this information can jeopardize employment and insurability. However, it is likely that the need for anonymity will disappear rapidly as laws to protect people from such discrimination are passed and enforced.

At the present time, all cases of AIDS must be reported to one or more governmental health agencies, but there is wide variation in what is done when a simple test for AIDS antibodies is positive. In some locations, the identity of people with positive tests must be reported to the public health authorities. In most cities and states, such reporting is not required yet. However, legislation is pending in many states that would require these reports, and it is not likely to be long before reporting is mandatory in all states. Ironically, every state in the Union already requires that positive tests for syphilis and gonorrhea be reported, though neither of these diseases comes anywhere near AIDS in terms of its threat to personal or public health.

One function of case reporting is to alert public health officials to the magnitude of the problem they are facing with any infectious disease. Another purpose is to facilitate "contact tracing." This is the process by which all past sexual contacts of an infected person are located by public health officers, are advised of the possibility that they could also be infected, and are tested to determine if that has, in fact, happened. Formal contact tracing for AIDS is now being done only in a few areas of the country, but pressure is mounting to mandate this activity on a nationwide basis.

Some people oppose mandatory reporting of positive antibody tests for AIDS out of fear that contact tracing will expose infected individuals to liability and discrimination. However, these arguments have not been sufficient to prevent reporting and tracing for many other infectious diseases. It remains to be seen what policies will be implemented with respect to AIDS.

THE COST OF TESTING

The cost of AIDS testing varies greatly from place to place (although all of the laboratories pay about the same price for the basic test kit—$6.50). In San Francisco, the price range is $20 to $80. In Los Angeles, private physicians and hospitals charge $40 to $150. (These costs include all of the retesting necessary if the original test is positive.)

WHAT OTHER TESTS CAN BE DONE?

Blood culture tests can be performed to try to detect the presence of the AIDS virus itself. However, this process is not likely to add any information that will change your medical care or the way you conduct your personal life. If the presence of AIDS antibodies in your blood has been confirmed with the Western Blot test, you must assume that the AIDS virus is also present in your blood (and in other body fluids). The culture tests are slow and expensive, and are primarily of value as a research tool.

Another test measures the number of T-helper cells in the blood. As an AIDS infection progresses, the number of these cells declines, and the body's resistance to disease decreases. A T-helper cell count of less than 200 cells per cubic millimeter indicates a great chance that a person who has been infected with the AIDS virus will go on to develop the full-blown disease of AIDS.

In one study at UCLA, 60 percent of ARC patients whose cell counts were this low developed AIDS within nine months. Among similar patients whose cell counts were over 350, only 10 percent experienced progression of their disease.

It is possible that the T-helper cell count may be valuable in identifying people who should be treated with drugs like AZT *before* their immune systems break down totally and life-threatening complications arise. More research is needed before we know whether the benefits of earlier treatment with such drugs will outweigh the risks.

A new test (known as an "antigen" test) is being developed that tests for parts of the AIDS virus itself. This test turns positive much earlier than the antibody test now used. Once the antigen test is available, it may be possible to diagnose an AIDS infection within two weeks of contact with the virus. This test is expected to be available for general use in the near future.

Great caution will have to be used when interpreting the antigen test, since in most cases it remains positive for only short periods of time. Within three or four months of infection, the antigen begins to disappear from the blood (probably because it is neutralized by antibodies against the virus that are now building up). Therefore, the antigen test will give a false negative result if it is used too late in a person who is infected with the AIDS virus.

WHERE *NOT* TO GET AN *AIDS* TEST

You should never donate blood to a blood bank as a way to be tested for AIDS. This places an additional burden on an already overloaded system. It also endangers the lives of others if yours turns out to be one of those extremely rare cases in which an infected specimen of blood escapes detection because of a false negative result on the test.

CHAPTER SIX

If Your Test Is Confirmed Positive

The following material applies only to those people who have a *confirmed* positive test for AIDS antibodies. If you are not sure what a *confirmed* positive test is, please review the material in Chapter 5.

It's almost too horrible to think about, isn't it? But there are about 1.5 million Americans who would get a confirmed positive result if they were tested for AIDS antibodies, so it's appropriate to deal with the issue here.

If your test is *confirmed* positive, you must make the following assumptions:

1. It is almost certain that you have been infected with the AIDS virus, and you must base all further actions on the assumption that you have been.

2. You are almost certainly capable of spreading the virus to others through the exchange of body fluids. As best we know, unless a medical breakthrough occurs you will remain infectious for the rest of your life.

3. You are at risk for developing ARC and AIDS itself. It is difficult to tell whether or not that will occur, but we do know that the risk is higher if any of the following factors apply to you:

   • You have had intimate sexual contact or shared needles with someone in whom AIDS developed.
   • Your T-helper cell count is less than 200 per cubic millimeter.

In order to evaluate your risk, you will need expert advice and you may need additional testing. It is critical that you take the best possible care to protect your health and the health of those around you.

THE BEST YOU CAN DO FOR YOURSELF

There are no scientifically proven actions you can take to prevent the onset of AIDS itself, although in selected cases there may be value in using drugs (such as AZT) that may slow the growth of the AIDS virus. There are some steps that logically seem worthwhile in view of our current knowledge:

Get the best medical advice and care you can find. There is a wide range in the quality of care and advice being given to people who have AIDS or a positive test for AIDS antibodies. In part, this is because our knowledge about AIDS is expanding so rapidly that many doctors are unable to keep up with the new information.

The doctors most likely to be in touch with the latest advances are those who are treating the most cases. These doctors have an urgent need to know everything about AIDS, so they read every article they can find on the subject in medical journals. They also have an extremely good network for sharing information, and news travels quickly among them.

In rural areas and cities where AIDS cases are rare, it should not be surprising that many doctors are less informed about the disease. But there are exceptions to this rule, and one can find doctors in these locations who are experts on the subject, just as—conversely— there are physicians practicing in the hearts of San Francisco and New York who remain ignorant of important facts about AIDS.

It would be dishonest to ignore the fact that some doctors do not want to know about AIDS. For whatever reason—fear of the disease, disdain for the people who get the disease, or just plain selfishness —these doctors shut their eyes to AIDS, and they close their doors to the people who have it.

Even your own doctor may reject you upon learning

that you have tested positive for antibodies to the AIDS virus. We've heard several tales of people who had visited the same doctor for twenty years, only to be shunned after the test results came back.

If your test is positive, you have entered a time during which you can ill afford to have such a doctor, so find one who is able and willing to take care of your needs. If there is a major treatment or research center in your area where AIDS patients are being treated, this is a good place to start looking. You can also get help by calling an AIDS resource center in your area or one of the AIDS referral services listed in Chapter 7.

Do not expose yourself to the body fluids of anyone else who is infected with the AIDS virus, regardless of whether or not they have the actual disease. Studies suggest that your chance of progressing on to AIDS are increased by repeated exposures to the virus.

Do not let yourself be immunized with any vaccines that contain live viruses. Although the viruses used in these vaccines are safe for most people, anyone whose immune system is weakened may become extremely sick after being immunized with them. If you are planning a trip that would necessitate your receiving immunizations, you should consider foregoing the trip.

Take good care of yourself. Never will these words be more important than now, when you need every bit of natural resistance you can muster. Eat well (not necessarily a lot, but well-chosen foods). Get plenty of exercise and rest. Avoid the use of tobacco and drugs and the excessive use of alcohol. There is no scientific proof that any of these steps will alter the course of AIDS, but common sense tells us that they could be worthwhile.

Stress interferes with the way your immune system responds to any challenge. So try to reduce the stress in your life, and learn deep relaxation techniques to relieve the ill effects of the stress that remains. Will this really make a difference in the course of AIDS? No one knows, but this is a time when you want everything possible working for you.

Stay well-informed about new developments in AIDS research and treatment. Though we do not yet have a cure and may not have one for a while, the picture could change rapidly and dramatically.

Don't take chances with unproven and unauthorized remedies. With a disease like AIDS, it's hard to know which remedies might be capable of making it worse.

Don't do anything crazy. A small number of people with AIDS have committed suicide because they couldn't cope with the overwhelming nature of their illness. If you ever find yourself considering such an alternative, get help immediately. Call family, friends, your doctor, or one of the AIDS hotlines. Help is available. Suicide is not an answer, particularly as medical breakthroughs become more possible with every passing day.

Don't give up hope. It now appears that a significant percentage of people infected with the AIDS virus may never develop the real disease. Don't throw your life away, only to discover ten years from now that your worst fears never materialized.

THE BEST YOU CAN DO FOR OTHERS

When your test for AIDS antibodies is positive, you must begin to think of what that means to others, particularly those with whom you might have sex in the future, and those with whom you have already done so. In an ethical sense—and perhaps in a legal sense—you have certain obligations to all of these people.

You must inform any current or future sexual partners of the fact that your test is positive, since—no matter what you do to protect them —they have some risk of infection through intimate contact with you. (They are *not* at risk, however, through non-sexual contact.) In my opinion, no one has the right to expose another person to a life-and-death situation without informing him or her of the risk beforehand. It's possible that your partner may decide to abstain completely from sexual activity with you. It's your partner's right to make that decision, just as it would be yours if the situation were reversed. It's also possible that a relationship that is very important to you could end over this issue. If so, that's the risk you'll have to take for being honest with your partner. A relationship based on dishonesty isn't worth anything anyway.

Aside from the purely ethical grounds for this position, there may be good legal grounds also. Although no legal precedent exists yet, a number of situations around the country have raised the issue of the responsibility for informing others of one's infection with the AIDS virus.

Lawsuits are already being filed against people who failed to tell their lovers that they had AIDS. It is hard to know how the courts will rule on this subject, but it is clear that those who fail to inform the people they place at risk could be in for some lengthy, expensive, and emotionally trying legal battles.

Few, if any, would argue with the moral obligation to let certain other people know that your test for AIDS antibodies is positive. The list would include anyone whose contact with you might involve the exchange of body fluids.

If ethical and legal grounds aren't enough for you, consider the story of the San Francisco man who murdered his male prostitute sex partner when the prostitute admitted—*after* they had sex—that he had AIDS. (The court reduced the charge from first- to second-degree murder.) Or the case of the Long Island man who stabbed a homosexual acquaintance in the neck when the man admitted that he was infected—again, *after* they had sex. (A sympathetic judge reduced the charge from murder to manslaughter. As a result, the killer will receive a much lighter sentence than would have been handed down for the original charge of murder.)

Don't engage in behaviors that expose others to a life-threatening illness. Regardless of the risks others are willing to take, I believe that each of us has an obligation not to infect others. Abstinence from any activity that exposes your partner to your body fluids is the only way to guarantee that you won't pass on the AIDS virus.

Notify all prior partners of your *confirmed* positive test and recommend that they be tested too. If they are infected, this will give them an opportunity to get the best kind of medical care and counseling at a very early stage. It should also motivate them to stop their sexual contacts with others.

If you are a woman, and you and your partner choose to continue having sexual intercourse, talk to your doctor about using oral contraceptives (birth control pills) *in addition* to condoms for contraception. It's important to consider this for two reasons: your baby would have an extremely great chance of being infected during pregnancy or childbirth, and pregnancy may make you more vulnerable to coming down with the final stage of AIDS. Pregnancy interferes with the immune response in normal women, and—in theory at least—creates an additional hazard for the woman infected with the AIDS virus. In one study of fifteen infected women who appeared well at the time of their deliveries, only three were free of symptoms thirty months later. Five of the women developed AIDS, and seven developed AIDS-related conditions.

If you are already pregnant, talk to your doctor about the options available to you for managing this pregnancy. Because of the risks described above, some doctors are recommending that abortion be considered. This is an issue that only you can decide.

Do not donate blood. Even with our new tests for screening blood donations, there is a very slight chance that the test will miss the fact that your blood contains AIDS virus antibodies. Giving blood when your test is positive is like playing Russian roulette. In this case, the gun is pointed at someone else's head.

Do not share hypodermic needles with anyone else. The sharing of needles by IV drug abusers is the second largest reason for the spread of AIDS today.

Don't share personal items such as razors or toothbrushes with other people. As best we know, no one has ever contracted AIDS this way, but—at least in theory—it's possible.

Tell your doctor and dentist about your test results. They need this information so that if problems develop, they can recognize them early. They also have a right to know for their own protection and the protection of their employees.

Your dentist is bound to come in contact with your saliva and will probably want to wear gloves and, perhaps, a mask during future examinations. Your doctor may need to draw blood or perform tests on stool and urine specimens. Knowing that your AIDS antibody test was positive will ensure that proper precautions are taken in his or her office and in laboratories where the specimens may be sent.

Tell the people you love, but be selective. Some of your family and friends—you can probably guess which ones—will be able to accept this situation and will give you the unqualified love, acceptance, and support that you need at this time. They are the ones you should turn to first. There will be others who cannot accept what you have to tell them, and whose reactions will make you feel worse. These are the people you may never want to tell.

Don't try to handle this situation alone. Perhaps more than at any other time in your life, you need the support and help of others. Take it, and give back what you can. The real meaning of life is found in the sharing and caring relationships we have with each other. That should not change just because an antibody test for AIDS is positive.

CHAPTER SEVEN

Counseling and Support Services

People with AIDS-related problems have a never-ending need for accurate information, counseling, medical services, and support. An extraordinary system for providing such services has developed rapidly, thanks primarily to the efforts of dedicated individuals working through community health organizations.

If you have questions about AIDS, or need help in obtaining AIDS-related services, you should first try to identify such an organization in your community. You can usually locate these groups by checking the phone book, asking telephone information, or calling your physician or local health department. If you have difficulty, contact one of the organizations listed at the end of this chapter.

COUNSELING

Because we had heard that the quality of counseling services varied around the country, I asked one of our researchers to call some of them anonymously and see what responses she got. She called telephone information in several large cities and small towns and simply asked for help in finding a counseling service that dealt with AIDS. In every case, friendly operators quickly provided her with a phone number.

Most of the time, that number connected her directly with an organization that was qualified to discuss AIDS. In the few instances when that did not happen, the person she reached was able to direct her promptly to the correct number.

Once she reached a counselor, she told the following story:

> *I've been going with this guy for a couple of months. We've never had sex, but last night we talked about it, and he told me he had tested positive for the AIDS virus. Now I need to know if it's really possible to have "safe sex."*

Every counselor with whom our researcher spoke was sincere and supportive. Each was willing to spend as much time as necessary and provide her with as much information as she wanted. However, while the nature of the communication was consistently warm and caring, the quality of the information supplied was uneven and, in some cases, inaccurate.

All of the counselors with whom she spoke agreed that the safest sex is so-called "dry sex," in which no body fluids are exchanged. This category includes caressing, massage, cuddling, hugging, closed-mouth kissing, and watching sexy movies together. A few counselors included some "wet" activities in this category, such as mutual masturbation and open-mouthed kissing, but provided no warning that the virus is present in saliva and semen.

In Kansas City, a counselor named Joe informed our researcher that using a condom was the only way to have "safe sex." In the next breath, he confided that the condom might break. We were alarmed by the way Joe explained the significance of the positive test our researcher's "boyfriend" had for AIDS antibodies. "There's no way to know if he really has the virus itself," he said. "It's possible that you could get it from him, but only 20 percent of the people exposed to it get it." We have no idea where Joe got this "fact." We hope he'll stop sharing such misinformation with others.

In Salt Lake City, the counselor who answered the phone described "safe sex" as sex with a condom. But, she asked, "Would you use a condom to protect yourself from getting pregnant?" She said that *she* wouldn't, and left our researcher with the impression that she probably shouldn't either.

To our horror, this same young woman told our researcher that it is difficult to pick up the AIDS virus through vaginal sex. Vaginal fluid, she said, is acidic and can kill the virus, so "it is nearly impossible for a woman to infect a man." The truth is that vaginal transmission from women to men has been clearly documented. It is believed that in Africa millions of men may have been infected this way.

The counselor who answered the Twin Cities Hotline in Minnesota was extremely well-informed. She and several others to whom we spoke described three categories of sexual behavior: "safe," "possibly safe," and "unsafe." She offered some interesting new ideas for safe sex, for example, each partner using his own dildo (no sharing allowed).

However, her "possibly safe" category contained one activity that we intensely dispute: oral sex, if the penis is withdrawn before ejaculation. Even if you could rely on your partner to withdraw his penis in time, the AIDS virus is almost certain to enter the mouth through pre-ejaculate fluids.

"Would *you* risk having sex with someone who tested positive?" our researcher asked this counselor. "I would if I really wanted to and followed the guidelines carefully," she responded, "but I would forego it if the relationship wasn't very important to me." In my opinion, this was a question the counselor had no business answering. A caller's decisions should be based on the facts, and should not be subject to the personal values of whichever counselor happens to answer the phone.

A counselor in Boston was well-informed and accurate in the advice she gave. She expressed special concern about the possibility of conception, and pointed out the high risk of AIDS in babies born to women who are infected (of the thirteen babies born in Boston with AIDS, eleven have died). She offered to send written material, promising that our researcher's identity would be protected by the destruction of her name and address as soon as the material was mailed.

To test the system further, we asked a young man to call some AIDS counseling services and present the following story:

> *I am bisexual and I have just tested positive for AIDS antibodies. Do I have to tell my girlfriend that I'm positive? Couldn't I just practice "safe sex"? Can I be sure that she won't get the virus?*

A counselor in Palm Beach told him that he would not infect his girlfriend if he wore a condom and used spermicide. But he was firm in his advice that she had to be told about the positive test beforehand. The counselor was sympathetic—he knew it would be difficult—but felt the girlfriend had a right to be told. In another piece of good advice, he also recommended that all prior sexual partners, male and female, be told about the test too.

In summary, we found that counseling is available everywhere in the country, but the expertise of the counselors is uneven and the advice not always reliable. I'd recommend that you use these counselors and resource centers to find printed information about AIDS and for referrals to testing centers, treatment facilities, and sources of social or financial support. For medical advice, I would seek out physicians and other health professionals who are properly trained and actively involved in the treatment of people with AIDS.

The following organizations have indicated a willingness to respond to all calls for help. If they are unable to solve your particular problem, they will assist you in finding someone who can.

TELEPHONE HOTLINES

PUBLIC HEALTH SERVICE
(PHS) HOTLINE
1-800-342-AIDS

This toll-free national hotline is operated by the American Social Health Association. It consists of a four-minute taped message, which explains how the AIDS virus is transmitted, how to prevent the spread of AIDS, and how to get tested for the presence of antibodies to the AIDS virus. At the end of the message, callers wanting additional information are referred to a toll-free number manned by live operators. That number is: 1-800-342-7514.

NATIONAL SEXUALLY TRANSMITTED DISEASES
HOTLINE
1-800-227-8922

This hotline answers questions about all sexually transmitted diseases. Questions about AIDS are referred to the PHS Hotline.

NATIONAL GAY TASK FORCE AIDS INFORMATION
HOTLINE
1-800-221-7044

This toll-free national hotline provides:

- information on all AIDS-related questions,
- counseling for AIDS patients,
- referrals all over the United States to physicians who specialize in treating AIDS and AIDS-related problems,

- referrals to AIDS support groups on a regional basis,
- referrals to sites for blood testing in all fifty states.

AIDS PROJECT LOS ANGELES
1362 Santa Monica Boulevard
Los Angeles, California 90046
1-213-876-2437

Although this organization primarily serves southern California, the hotline gets calls from all over the country and is able to tell people where to seek information and help in their own areas. The Project offers a comprehensive range of services to AIDS patients and their families, including counseling, in-home assistance, shelter, a food distribution program, support groups, dental care, legal services, and drug and alcohol abuse counseling. The Project does not operate its own test center, but makes appropriate referrals.

This organization operates the following toll-free numbers:

- for Los Angeles only: 1-213-876-AIDS
- for southern California: 1-800-992-AIDS
- for the hearing impaired: 1-800-553-AIDS
- for Spanish-speaking people: 1-800-222-SIDA

SAN FRANCISCO AIDS FOUNDATION
333 Valencia Street
4th floor
San Francisco, California 94103
1-800-FOR-AIDS

This organization primarily serves northern California, but handles inquiries from all over the country. The toll-free hotline provides information, counseling, and referral to physicians, test sites, and support groups. The Foundation also offers a catalogue of printed materials on AIDS. These materials are available at no cost to AIDS patients and their families. There is a small charge to others. To order the catalogue, call: 1-415-861-3397.

INFORMATION SOURCES

NATIONAL AIDS NETWORK
729 Eighth Street, S.E.
Suite 300
Washington, D.C. 20003
1-202-347-0390

This is a clearinghouse for printed materials and video programs on AIDS that serves individuals and organizations. The materials range from basic information for lay people to technical and medical information for health care providers. The network also has a directory of 275 AIDS health care providers throughout the U.S.

NATIONAL COALITION OF HISPANIC HEALTH AND
HUMAN SERVICES (COSSMHO)
1030 15th Street, N.W.
Suite 1053
Washington, D.C. 20005
1-202-371-2100

COSSMHO is a nationwide network of Hispanics involved in AIDS health care. It also has a National Directory of AIDS services for Hispanics. The Coalition is funded by the Department of Health and Human Services and by corporate contributions.

THE FUND FOR HUMAN DIGNITY
666 Broadway
4th floor
New York, New York 10012

This organization offers printed materials on the general subject of AIDS, and specific recommendations for those whose AIDS antibody tests are positive. The organization asks for a $1 donation with each request, to help cover costs.

THE AMERICAN RED CROSS
National AIDS Education Office
1730 D Street, N.W.
Washington, D.C. 20006
1-202-737-8300

The Red Cross supplies educational materials on AIDS to teachers, community group leaders, or any individual conducting AIDS education programs. Any of the 3,000 chapters of the Red Cross can provide the materials, which include a video documentary and various brochures. The emphasis of this information is on AIDS prevention.

AIDS ACTION COUNCIL
729 Eighth Street, S.E.
Suite 200
Washington, D.C. 20003
1-202-547-3101

The Council is made up of about 250 organizations which provide AIDS-related services around the United States. The primary function of this organization is lobbying the U.S. government for funding for AIDS service providers. Callers are referred to their nearest member provider (there is at least one Council member in every state in the U.S.). A monthly newsletter published by the Council reports on the progress being made with lobbying efforts.

SUPPORT GROUPS

MOTHERS OF AIDS PATIENTS (MAP)
3403 E Street
San Diego, California 92101
1-619-234-3432

This organization provides emotional support and group therapy for AIDS patients and their immediate family members all over the country (especially in areas like the Midwest and South, where it is difficult to find support). MAP distributes information for families of newly diagnosed AIDS patients and assists these families in forming local support groups.

VOLUNTEER ORGANIZATIONS

SHANTI FOUNDATION
9060 Santa Monica Boulevard
Suite 301
West Hollywood, California 90069
1-213-273-7591

The Foundation operates separate but related groups in Los Angeles and San Francisco. It offers emotional support services to people who have AIDS by providing a "buddy" or companion who becomes a real friend, someone to turn to when things get rough.

There are volunteer services like these in many cities. Any AIDS Hotline could make a referral.

RESEARCH ORGANIZATIONS

AMERICAN FOUNDATION FOR AIDS RESEARCH
9601 Wilshire Boulevard
Los Angeles, California 90210-5294
1-213-273-5547

The American Foundation for AIDS Research (AmFAR) is a nonprofit organization dedicated to advancing and funding research on AIDS. It also funds the development of educational programs and serves as a resource for responsible information on the clinical, biological, psychosocial, public health, and public policy aspects of AIDS. The Foundation receives its support from private donations.

Epilogue

During the next few years, hundreds of thousands of people will die of AIDS. Short of a miracle, there is little any of us can do to keep that from happening. But there are things we *can* do to ease the burden of human suffering and keep this dreadful scene from repeating itself. We must reach out to those who are infected with the AIDS virus, so they know that they are not alone. With time and money, and with our hearts, we must support the community organizations that have worked so hard and so unselfishly for the victims of AIDS. Their labor has just begun.

We must demand that our government give greater financial and political support to AIDS research and services. We must stop pretending that we can't afford it. Hundreds of thousands of young Americans will die of AIDS while we spend hundreds of billions of dollars on the weapons of war.

LOOKING TO THE FUTURE
Incidence of AIDS in the United States and Associated Mortality*

		# of Cases Diagnosed During Year	# of Deaths During Year
Actual	1981	321	146
Actual	1982	1,002	382
Actual	1983	2,736	1,225
Actual	1984	5,456	2,829
Actual	1985	8,775	5,178
Projected	1986	15,800	9,000
Projected	1987	23,000	14,000
Projected	1988	33,000	21,000
Projected	1989	45,000	30,000
Projected	1990	58,000	41,000
Projected	1991	74,000	54,000

We must practice safer sex. Unsafe sexual activity is now the primary mechanism for spreading the AIDS virus. This is the area over which each of us has the most control. Armed with an accurate appreciation of this deadly disease and how it is spread, we must do better sexually to stop it.

Always the optimist, I believe that we can do better. We've got to do better. It's the only way to save each other.

*Public Health Service Reports, September–October, 1986.

About the Author

Dr. Art Ulene is best known as "Family Doctor" of NBC's "Today" show, where his more than 1,000 health advisories have guided millions of viewers to better health. His syndicated medical report, "Feeling Fine," is a regular feature of newscasts in more than one hundred cities in the United States and several foreign countries. He is a Board-certified obstetrician/gynecologist, a clinical associate professor at the University of Southern California School of Medicine, and a member of the Board of Trustees of the Norris/USC Cancer Center. He lives in Los Angeles with his wife, Priscilla, who works with him to produce educational programs for several major medical organizations. They have three children: Douglas, 25; Valerie, 22; and Steven, 20.